Multi-Dimensional Diversification: Improving Portfolio Selection Using Principal Component Analysis

Rufus Rankin, DBA

Copyright © 2016 Rufus G. Rankin

All rights reserved.

ISBN: 153317850X
ISBN-13: 978-1533178503

CONTENTS

	Acknowledgments	i
	Introduction	1
1	Correlation Challenges	Pg 3
2	Introducing PCA	Pg 8
3	Putting PCA to Work	Pg 15
4	Rotation and Stability	Pg 32
5	Implementation	Pg 39
	Conclusion and Summary	Pg 46
	Appendices	Pg 47

ACKNOWLEDGMENTS

First and foremost Ana, for everything.

My colleagues at Equinox, especially (but not limited to) Ajay, Bob and John.

Steven Lerit for the encouragement, detailed questions and suggestions (including the equity factor analogy idea).

Professor Mark Salmon, Dr. Wes Gray and Mebane Faber for general comradery and specific feedback.

INTRODUCTION

In the 1960s, researchers like William Sharpe created the Capital Asset Pricing Model to help make sense of modeling stock returns by relating an individual equity to the "market" as a proxy for systematic risk. This provided a single-factor model for explaining equity returns. In the 1990s, Fama and French proposed a three-factor model, adding Size and Value as additional explanatory variables for stock returns after observing that small stocks often outperform large stocks and cheap stocks often outperform expensive stocks. Carhart then added Momentum as a fourth factor after researchers noticed that over medium time frames, winners tend to keep winning (and losers tend to keep losing); now, we have many more factors than that.

These factors play an important part in selecting stocks and analyzing the returns of equity managers, and a big part of their helpfulness lies in their ability to simplify the numerous return drivers available within the stock market. Consider the S&P 500: you can analyze each stock in the index endlessly, but by using one of these factor models, you can quickly sort and simplify 500 stocks into a few basic categories, such as "Value" or "Growth" stocks.

But, what if you don't happen to be a Nobel Prize-winning researcher in Economic Sciences? These classic factors were developed over a few decades of research and derived from a great deal of observation and testing, so unless you're Bill Sharpe (and if you are, thanks for reading my book!), it might be helpful to find additional options for identifying factors or risk drivers.

We can use Principal Component Analysis (PCA)—a type of dimension reduction—to boil almost any set of investment returns into a few factors that explain most of what is going on in the data set. The best part is that software does all of the work in identifying the factors. The worst part is that you sometimes have to figure out what those factors *mean* on your own.

In this book, I will show you how to use PCA to identify the main risk drivers in simple multiasset portfolios (i.e., Stock, Bond, Real Estate, etc.). From there, it is my hope that you will be able to extend the use of PCA into whatever asset class or set of asset classes you work with.

This book is not meant to be an exhaustive review of principal component analysis. Nor is it meant to be entirely academically rigorous. While there are plenty of academic resources on principal component analysis (suggested resources are provided at the end of this book), they tend to be very complicated in approach and rather narrow in scope. There is not, to my knowledge, a straight-forward explanation of how professionals in the investment management industry can put PCA to work in their daily practice. PCA is a powerful tool that can identify risk drivers in a group of assets—some of which may not be intuitive or obvious. While it seems to be quite complicated, in fact, PCA can be simple to implement and may be well worth the time and effort.

There's an oft-repeated phrase to the effect that diversification is the only free lunch in finance. I'm not sure I agree. It takes work and research to achieve a meaningful degree of diversification, especially when investing within a single asset class. For me, diversification should first and most importantly reduce the risk of catastrophic loss. Once that has been achieved to a reasonable level of satisfaction (there are no guarantees), then we can look for additional benefits such as reducing portfolio volatility and even boosting returns. All investors make mistakes from time to time, and unexpected bad luck will play a part at some point in almost any investor's career. As I am writing this (2015), we have seen many surprises in the markets, including the Swiss National (central) Bank unpegging the CHF from the Euro and a massive short-term decline in the Chinese stock market. A healthy level of diversification may help protect against a wide array of mistakes and unfortunate events such as these.

My goal for this book is to provide you with the information to decide if PCA might be helpful in your practice and, if so, to arm you with the knowledge to begin using it.

1 CORRELATION CHALLENGES

Correlation Matrices

Diversification is difficult. An analyst can do a lot of research into different assets or investments and still wind up with a portfolio that is heavily exposed to fewer risks than is optimal. A simple shotgun approach to diversification (i.e., just buy as many assets as possible) certainly isn't an optimal solution as you can easily overallocate capital to a small number of risk drivers and overspend in transaction costs without generating any meaningful benefit. Factor analysis, style analysis, and correlation analysis are helpful tools, but each has its challenges. While a correlation or covariance matrix can be helpful, once you start looking at more than 10 or so assets, it can become very complex and unwieldy.

Consider the correlation matrix for 10 assets. Using color coding in Figure 1, the strongest relationships are green, and the weakest relationships (negative correlations) are red. Please ignore the diagonals, which are ones.

	A	B	C	D	E	F	G	H	I	J
A	1.000	0.224	0.142	0.296	0.090	0.495	0.328	0.601	0.554	-0.098
B	0.224	1.000	0.305	0.092	0.144	0.272	0.055	0.411	0.260	-0.056
C	0.142	0.305	1.000	0.089	0.170	0.213	0.063	0.335	0.205	0.076
D	0.296	0.092	0.089	1.000	0.203	0.249	0.444	0.239	0.238	0.139
E	0.090	0.144	0.170	0.203	1.000	0.191	0.128	0.340	0.265	0.020
F	0.495	0.272	0.213	0.249	0.191	1.000	0.470	0.587	0.559	-0.028
G	0.328	0.055	0.063	0.444	0.128	0.470	1.000	0.300	0.357	0.237
H	0.601	0.411	0.335	0.239	0.340	0.587	0.300	1.000	0.591	-0.111
I	0.554	0.260	0.205	0.238	0.265	0.559	0.357	0.591	1.000	0.014
J	-0.098	-0.056	0.076	0.139	0.020	-0.028	0.237	-0.111	0.014	1.000

Figure 1. Correlation matrix of 10 investments

A quick formula for figuring out the number of pairwise combinations in a correlation matrix is $(N(N-1))/2$. For 10 assets, that would be $(10(10-1))/2 = 45$ combinations. Not too bad, as we can get some ideas about which assets are similar, at least during the window of analysis.

Are we really likely to only consider 10 investments at a time? To me, that seems like a rather small universe to consider even if you only plan to invest in a handful of assets. In my own work, I tend to look at from 30 to 50 potential investments at a time; so, let's try the above exercise with 30 investments (Figure 2). What does that look like?

Multi-Dimensional Diversification

	A	B	C	D	E	F	G	H	I	J	K	L	M	N	O	P	Q	R	S	T	U
A	1.000	0.224	0.142	0.296	0.090	0.495	0.328	0.601	0.554	-0.098	0.440	0.544	0.509	0.491	0.665	0.668	0.408	0.558	0.624	0.543	0.31
B	0.224	1.000	0.305	0.092	0.144	0.272	-0.055	0.411	0.260	-0.056	0.214	0.282	0.230	0.133	0.217	0.253	0.182	0.084	0.214	0.237	0.06
C	0.142	0.305	1.000	0.089	0.170	0.213	0.063	0.335	0.205	0.076	0.184	0.147	0.101	0.194	0.194	0.165	0.057	0.202	0.176	0.210	0.02
D	0.296	0.092	0.089	1.000	0.203	0.249	0.444	0.239	0.238	0.139	0.396	0.440	0.451	0.484	0.425	0.349	0.332	0.438	0.453	0.367	0.46
E	0.090	0.144	0.170	0.203	1.000	0.191	0.128	0.340	0.265	0.020	0.311	0.248	0.264	0.286	0.190	0.202	0.235	0.188	0.237	0.256	0.13
F	0.495	0.272	0.213	0.249	0.191	1.000	0.470	0.587	0.559	-0.028	0.695	0.603	0.483	0.620	0.568	0.679	0.550	0.617	0.467	0.698	0.31
G	0.328	-0.055	0.063	0.444	0.128	0.470	1.000	0.300	0.357	0.237	0.434	0.493	0.462	0.484	0.470	0.456	0.386	0.438	0.435	0.459	0.38
H	0.601	0.411	0.335	0.239	0.340	0.587	0.300	1.000	0.591	-0.114	0.583	0.544	0.471	0.533	0.610	0.692	0.408	0.537	0.506	0.667	0.23
I	0.554	0.260	0.205	0.238	0.265	0.559	0.357	0.591	1.000	0.014	0.564	0.568	0.566	0.510	0.566	0.637	0.271	0.572	0.545	0.636	0.38
J	-0.098	-0.056	0.076	0.139	0.020	-0.028	0.237	-0.111	0.014	1.000	-0.001	0.031	0.068	0.029	0.009	-0.074	-0.009	-0.001	0.072	0.002	0.13
K	0.440	0.214	0.184	0.396	0.311	0.695	0.434	0.583	0.564	-0.001	1.000	0.589	0.558	0.689	0.557	0.602	0.582	0.663	0.557	0.748	0.42
L	0.544	0.282	0.147	0.440	0.248	0.603	0.493	0.544	0.568	0.031	0.589	1.000	0.593	0.604	0.668	0.677	0.491	0.650	0.588	0.619	0.36
M	0.509	0.230	0.101	0.451	0.264	0.483	0.462	0.471	0.566	0.068	0.558	0.593	1.000	0.509	0.641	0.597	0.430	0.493	0.722	0.525	0.45
N	0.491	0.133	0.194	0.484	0.286	0.620	0.484	0.533	0.510	0.029	0.689	0.604	0.509	1.000	0.612	0.623	0.613	0.671	0.536	0.675	0.42
O	0.665	0.217	0.194	0.425	0.190	0.568	0.470	0.610	0.566	0.557	0.668	0.641	1.000	0.612	1.000	0.710	0.437	0.698	0.799	0.698	0.40
P	0.668	0.253	0.165	0.349	0.202	0.679	0.456	0.692	0.637	-0.074	0.602	0.677	0.597	0.623	0.710	1.000	0.484	0.681	0.604	0.712	0.35
Q	0.408	0.182	0.057	0.332	0.235	0.550	0.386	0.408	0.271	-0.009	0.582	0.491	0.430	0.613	0.437	0.484	1.000	0.487	0.425	0.511	0.28
R	0.558	0.084	0.202	0.438	0.188	0.617	0.438	0.537	0.572	-0.001	0.663	0.650	0.493	0.671	0.698	0.681	0.487	1.000	0.607	0.696	0.33
S	0.624	0.214	0.176	0.453	0.237	0.467	0.435	0.506	0.545	0.072	0.557	0.588	0.722	0.536	0.799	0.604	0.425	0.607	1.000	0.612	0.49
T	0.543	0.237	0.210	0.367	0.256	0.698	0.459	0.667	0.636	0.002	0.748	0.619	0.525	0.675	0.698	0.712	0.511	0.696	0.612	1.000	0.42
U	0.319	0.065	0.028	0.464	0.139	0.315	0.382	0.234	0.386	0.132	0.427	0.364	0.454	0.422	0.409	0.358	0.280	0.333	0.491	0.420	1.00
V	0.032	-0.153	-0.038	0.142	-0.013	0.141	0.214	-0.033	0.047	0.226	0.192	0.095	0.129	0.160	0.181	0.050	0.142	0.180	0.116	0.168	0.06
W	0.604	0.361	0.242	0.348	0.273	0.668	0.461	0.716	0.642	-0.003	0.631	0.677	0.669	0.583	0.833	0.756	0.494	0.674	0.763	0.756	0.39
X	0.088	0.068	0.176	0.100	0.070	-0.034	-0.040	0.164	0.080	0.113	0.024	-0.014	-0.012	-0.009	0.036	0.031	-0.097	0.003	0.139	-0.013	-0.01
Y	0.011	0.137	0.376	-0.047	0.196	0.141	0.183	0.193	0.211	0.084	0.093	0.111	0.041	0.131	0.040	0.107	-0.093	0.122	0.083	0.192	0.04
Z	0.543	0.180	0.226	0.265	0.378	0.408	0.288	0.528	0.525	0.023	0.455	0.547	0.563	0.384	0.605	0.523	0.355	0.454	0.671	0.500	0.29
AA	0.526	0.076	0.133	0.471	0.158	0.516	0.508	0.435	0.453	0.022	0.621	0.569	0.522	0.648	0.694	0.644	0.452	0.676	0.650	0.627	0.49
BB	0.645	0.294	0.257	0.424	0.304	0.494	0.340	0.668	0.613	-0.001	0.512	0.583	0.573	0.561	0.691	0.681	0.415	0.618	0.672	0.604	0.34
CC	0.594	0.161	0.183	0.370	0.173	0.654	0.455	0.602	0.637	-0.012	0.594	0.658	0.622	0.626	0.737	0.737	0.447	0.652	0.662	0.728	0.40
DD	0.568	0.299	0.175	0.367	0.187	0.499	0.323	0.508	0.532	0.039	0.606	0.597	0.554	0.591	0.598	0.580	0.430	0.566	0.625	0.611	0.41

Figure 2. Correlation matrix of 30 investments.

Figure 2 is certainly more complicated, not to mention difficult to even read. Using the previous formula, we now have (30(30-1))/2, or 435 combinations. We can easily calculate that we would be looking at 1,225 combinations with 50 assets and 4,950 when looking at 100 assets. At somewhere between 50 and 100, your computer may start to slow down and the output may not be particularly helpful. Therefore, it might be best to use correlation matrices for digging into smaller samples once the opportunity set has been narrowed down.

Correlations Change

Another challenge when using correlations is that they tend to fluctuate through time. Keeping an eye on rolling correlations and how they shift through time can help, but if we have a multiasset portfolio to create and take one correlation "snapshot" (i.e., use a single time window), we could be way off in terms of some of the relationships we capture. An important relationship analysts often look at is the correlation between stocks and bonds. We can look at the relationship between SPY, an ETF that tracks the S&P 500, and IEF, an ETF that tracks 7- to 10-year US Treasury Bonds.

Table 1
Six-month Correlation

	Six-month Correlation SPY & IEF
Average	-0.3406
Highest	0.2453
Lowest	-0.7765
Negative	86%
% > Avg.	45%

The period of analysis runs from late 2002 until July of 2015. Using daily returns, we see in Table 1 the average rolling 132-day (roughly six months of trading days) correlation between SPY and IEF is -0.3406—a mildly significant negative correlation. We can also see that the rolling correlation has peaked at 0.24 and has dropped as low as -0.77. The correlation has been negative approximately 86% of the time during this window of observation, and the rolling correlation was above the long-run average of -0.3406 approximately 45% of the time.

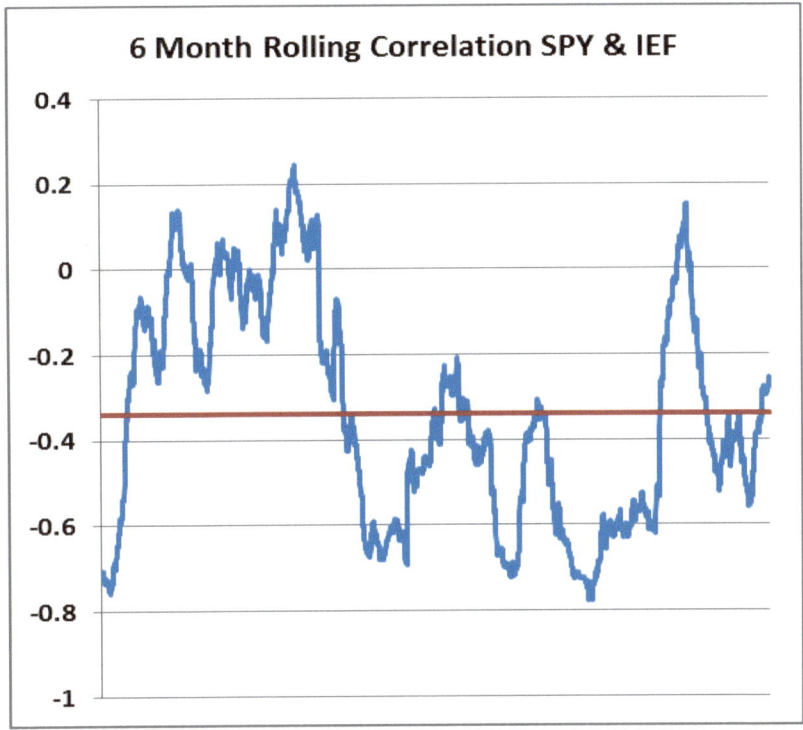

Figure 3. Six-month rolling correlation between SPY and IEF

In Figure 3, we can see clearly that the rolling correlation shifts around a great deal, and I can tell you that translating this information into a robust investment or trading process has bedeviled some very clever minds in our industry. While there is no straightforward lesson to be derived from this, I do hope you will note that correlations can fluctuate a great deal, and while minding one correlation metric is feasible, we may find it challenging to monitor the shifting relationships between many different assets. However, using PCA can help give us extra insight into the relationships between the assets in our portfolio.

2 INTRODUCING PCA

To recap: we are looking for an analysis that clearly and simply shows us the relationships within our universe of potential investments. PCA is just such a tool. In a few short steps, PCA can strip out the independent sources of return in a set of assets and show you which of those drivers each asset in your universe offers exposure. One simple table can show you the underlying drivers in your investment universe and which assets to allocate to in order to access those drivers.

Going back to the correlation table example, we can apply a PCA analysis to the same 30-asset universe. The output table has a different principal component for each column and shows each asset's loading or correlation with the component. We can see that assets A through P (about half of the sample) have high loadings on the first component, which means we should not expect them to provide meaningful diversification benefits relative to each other. The large number of assets loading on the first component also suggests that the first component represents the "market," or main source of return, in the universe we are examining. When we walk through the steps of PCA later on, we will see that is exactly what the first component represents: the largest source of variation in the data set.

We can also see that several assets "cluster" together, or load, on the same components. An important feature of PCA is that each principal component is completely orthogonal, or statistically independent, from each of the other components. That means that assets with a high loading on a particular component and little or no loading on other components can be considered independent of other assets.

While we will explore the details of the analysis shortly, it is useful to think of the first principal component as the "market," benchmark, or key driver for all of the assets considered. An analyst can probably significantly enhance the diversification of a portfolio just by adding assets with low to negative loadings on the first principal component without worrying overmuch about the meaning or specifics of the other components.

Table 2 shows a "Loading Matrix" for a PCA. The loading matrix shows how each variable or investment loads on a particular principal component. Each column represents one principal component, and each row represents an investment. Each of the numbers is the loading for an investment on that particular component. I will usually sort the table by the loadings on the first component.

Table 2
PCA Output for 30 Assets

	PC 1	PC 2	PC 3	PC 4	PC 5	PC 6	PC 7	PC 8
A	**0.836**	0.287	0.089	0.078	0.064	0.168	-0.026	0.088
B	**0.828**	0.256	0.187	-0.027	0.088	0.012	0.045	-0.033
C	**0.807**	0.083	0.329	-0.050	0.123	0.037	0.106	0.094
D	**0.774**	-0.007	0.009	-0.091	0.125	0.072	0.121	0.264
E	**0.768**	0.334	0.150	0.099	0.008	-0.040	-0.035	-0.035
F	**0.766**	0.179	0.097	-0.074	-0.133	0.072	0.121	-0.138
G	**0.760**	0.393	0.109	0.083	-0.099	0.057	-0.029	-0.032
H	**0.737**	0.141	0.076	0.260	-0.019	0.041	-0.064	0.128
I	**0.736**	0.215	0.191	0.119	-0.061	0.094	0.199	0.119
J	**0.708**	0.097	0.325	-0.092	0.161	0.118	-0.131	0.202
K	**0.666**	0.352	-0.066	0.177	-0.160	0.269	0.163	0.173
L	**0.658**	0.525	0.123	0.190	0.026	0.025	-0.066	0.058
M	**0.652**	0.361	0.230	0.033	0.066	0.149	-0.099	0.075
N	**0.620**	0.532	0.180	0.123	0.002	-0.139	0.053	-0.040
O	**0.610**	0.301	0.294	0.076	0.001	0.164	0.000	-0.008
P	**0.589**	0.446	0.365	0.036	0.094	-0.177	0.033	-0.093
Q	0.538	**0.620**	-0.003	0.150	0.044	0.149	-0.133	-0.009
R	0.493	**0.644**	0.196	0.065	0.048	0.052	-0.018	0.186
S	0.448	**0.660**	0.334	0.106	-0.002	-0.023	0.015	0.101
T	0.350	0.074	0.718	0.050	0.032	-0.039	-0.116	0.038
U	0.347	0.324	0.419	0.176	0.357	-0.024	-0.200	-0.039
V	0.299	**0.686**	0.146	-0.265	0.062	0.189	-0.084	0.174
W	0.222	0.087	-0.017	0.078	-0.057	**0.873**	0.021	0.023
X	0.216	0.290	**0.739**	-0.120	0.094	0.029	0.222	0.083
Y	0.154	0.159	0.077	0.136	-0.026	0.028	0.052	**0.913**
Z	0.129	0.149	-0.043	**0.542**	0.057	0.380	0.352	0.027
AA	0.082	-0.103	0.022	0.081	0.059	0.019	**0.870**	0.041
BB	0.078	-0.010	0.012	**0.890**	0.045	0.008	0.001	0.108
CC	0.076	0.321	-0.150	-0.104	**0.689**	-0.327	0.090	-0.053
DD	-0.055	-0.134	0.232	0.127	**0.786**	0.116	0.037	0.021

In Table 2, we can see which assets we can expect to behave in a similar fashion, such as A through P, and CC and DD. We can also see that assets such as X and W appear to be on their own and completely unrelated to the rest. Therefore, they may warrant further consideration as additions to a portfolio.

In addition to Table 2, which shows the loadings of each asset on the different principal components, we can also use a sample PCA output as shown in Table 3. The first row shows each of the principal components extracted—F1 through F5. This table shows how much of the total variation of the sample or investment universe each component explains (Variability %) and the cumulative amount of variation explained as you add components (Cumulative %). This output is helpful in a few ways, but most importantly it lets us know how many components explain meaningful amounts of variance which will help us figure out how many components to use and what the relative diversification level of our portfolio is.

Table 3
Sample PCA output

Components	F1	F2	F3	F4	F5
Eigenvalue	3.08	0.98	0.61	0.24	0.08
Variability (%)	61.68	19.65	12.25	4.75	1.67
Cumulative %	61.68	81.33	93.58	98.33	100.00

Now that I have shown you what PCA can do, in the next section, we will walk through the nuts and bolts of how PCA works.

PCA Explanation

Principal component analysis (PCA) is a type of factor analysis—a statistical method of dimension reduction that is used to reduce the complexity of a data set. This is accomplished by extracting factors or components that explain large portions of the variation in a sample of variables, and those factors are linear combinations of the variables. The key benefits of PCA are that it transforms the data into a more easily interpreted subset due to reduced dimensionality, and it expresses the data in terms of relationships between the variables or patterns in the data. PCA can uncover the primary patterns or structure hidden in a data set. These patterns are expressed as lines called eigenvectors, which the analysis presents as components. An important feature of PCA is that each component is orthogonal to the other (i.e., perpendicular in a geometric sense) and is completely independent of the others in a statistical sense.

Correlation and covariance analysis are two-dimensional: they can only describe the relationships between two variables at a time. PCA is multidimensional and can present the various relationships between numerous variables at once. Unlike traditional factor analysis, which compares the returns of an asset with various exogenous risk factors introduced by the analyst, PCA looks at the covariance or correlation matrix of variables—in our case, returns for various assets—and creates new factors or components that explain large percentages of the variation in the asset returns. For a data set of p variables, PCA will create a smaller k number of variables (Principal Components) that will explain a large portion of the total variation in the data set.

There are several exhaustive surveys of principal component analysis available, and I share a few resources in the Additional Resources at the end of this book. Next, we will review the steps of PCA. Although this is a bit dense, it is important to understand the basic procedure before proceeding with implementation.

PCA steps

PCA is a linear transformation that can reorient a data set according to the eigenvectors of the covariance or correlation matrix and map the data set into fewer dimensions. Typically, the data will be mean adjusted, so each variable or dimension will have a mean of zero. The correlation or covariance matrix of the adjusted data set is then created, and eigenvectors and eigenvalues are computed for the matrix. To be clear, the dimensions in this analysis are the columns of the covariance matrix, each column representing a single dimension. PCA can be very time consuming to perform by hand; fortunately, software packages can perform the analysis very quickly.

In this circumstance, the *eigenvector* represents the line along which a particular dimension would be plotted if graphed, and the *eigenvalue* represents the relative variance of the data set accounted for by that dimension. The eigenvector with the largest eigenvalue is the line or dimension that captures the greatest percentage of the total variance and becomes the first principal component. In the case of two variables, this would be analogous to the line of best fit or linear regression line. While the eigenvector describes the line or dimension, the eigenvalue represents the amount of variance described or captured by the eigenvector. An eigenvector (and accompanying eigenvalue) is calculated for each dimension, but a researcher will usually only retain a few of the eigenvectors because the main purpose of the analysis is to reduce the dimensionality of the data. There are no universally accepted standards for choosing how many to retain, but researchers will typically disregard eigenvectors with eigenvalues less than a certain threshold, such as 1, or once a certain threshold of total sample variance is reached, such as 75%. Ignoring eigenvectors with values less than 1 is known as Kaiser's Criterion, but this can be too restrictive depending on the sample, so Jolliffe's Criterion of .70 may be a better limit to avoid eliminating helpful components. Once the selected number of eigenvectors is retained, the original data set is transformed using the retained eigenvector matrix, which yields the final components.

A table exhibiting the correlations of each variable to the retained components, also known as factor or component loadings, makes the underlying patterns or relationships between the variables clearer. These patterns can be interpreted as payoffs or investment styles in the context of asset analysis and can be used to improve the diversification or tailor the exposure of a portfolio.

Data considerations

Data used for principal component analysis must be clean, and the variables must be reasonably well correlated. Furthermore, in order to perform a good analysis, sufficient observations for each of the variables are necessary. Many PCA packages will report a statistic called the Kaiser-Meyer-Olkin (KMO) measure of sampling adequacy. The KMO is used to indicate to a researcher whether the variables are correlated enough to be suitable for a principal component analysis. Technically speaking, the KMO represents the ratio of the squared correlation between variables to the squared partial correlation between variables, and it varies between 0 and 1. A score close to 0 indicates a large diffusion in the pattern of correlations, as the sum of partial correlations is large relative to the sum of correlations, which suggests that the data set is not suitable for factor analysis. Most researchers will not proceed with the analysis if the KMO is lower than 0.700, and they should either reduce the number of variables or increase the number of observations.

Correlation vs. covariance matrix

While PCA can be performed on a *covariance* matrix, it is more common to perform the analysis on the *correlation* matrix. The correlation matrix is essentially a standardized covariance matrix and can therefore be used for comparing variables in different units (e.g., gallons or degrees Fahrenheit) and prevents a small number of variables with higher variance than the others swaying the analysis. This can happen quite frequently when analyzing investments. Consider the relative variance of stocks vs. bonds, for example. Due to the standardization or scaling of the correlation matrix, each variable's variance is weighted equally. This is important when analyzing investments with large differences in variance because it prevents one or two investments with high variances from dominating the analysis. In most cases, better results will be obtained from the analysis by using correlations. The correlation matrix is used for all analyses described herein, unless explicitly stated otherwise.

To summarize, PCA is a type of factor analysis with the relatively unique feature of creating factors from the data set rather than applying exogenous factors to the analysis. By extracting endogenous factors, PCA can identify the main drivers or investment styles in a set of investment returns.

3 PUTTING PCA TO WORK

In this chapter, we are going to work through building an international, multiasset portfolio from scratch and see how we can use PCA to improve the diversification of the portfolio.

Defining Diversification

Before we go about trying to improve the diversification of a portfolio, we should come up with a working definition. Let's define diversification as the number of uncorrelated return sources or bets we have in the portfolio. I am not using correlation in the sense of having a Pearson correlation coefficient of zero between two assets; I am asking how many truly unrelated investments or risk drivers we have access to. That means that each risk driver or factor must be completely uncorrelated not just to one, but to all, of the other risk factors in the portfolio. Therefore, the more "uncorrelated bets" we have in the portfolio, the higher the level of diversification.

For example, are we enhancing diversification by using large cap growth and large cap value? Are they really that different? I would argue that large cap growth stocks and large cap value stocks are going to be very similar over the long run and might not count as uncorrelated bets, assuming we are talking about long-only investments (long/short portfolios that offer exposure to "value" or other factors while neutralizing market beta are another story). It may, and probably does, add value to include both in certain portfolios, but in terms of the broad asset mix when considering multiple asset classes, they are both offering the same risk driver. For now, we are going to focus on the multiasset portfolio.

Building a Portfolio

We will use 13 assets to replicate a broad multiasset portfolio that represents most of the investment options available. Those assets are listed in Table 4.

Table 4
List of Assets Used in Universe

Asset	Index	Tracker
US Equity	S&P 500	**SPY**
US Equity	Russell 2000 Small Cap	**IWM**
Real Estate	DJ US Real Estate Index	**IYR**
Real Estate	Fidelity International Real Estate Fund	**FIREX**
Non-US Equity	MSCI EAFE	**EFA**
Non-US Equity	MSCI Emerging Markets	**EEM**
Credit	Barclays US Aggregate Bond Index	**AGG**
Credit	Pimco Foreign Bond Fund	**PFORX**
Commodity	Bloomberg Commodity Index	**PCRIX**
Commodity	Gold	**GLD**
Alternative*	EurekaHedge Long/Short Equity	**Equity L/S**
Alternative*	EurekaHedge Event Driven	**Event Driven**
Alternative*	EurekaHedge CTA	**CTA**

*We use index data for alternatives.

Many analysts conflate the number of investments with the amount of diversification. For example, if I have 10 investments, I will likely believe that I am more diversified than if I have only five investments. The first task we will use PCA for is to measure the relative diversification of portfolios that we are considering. That way we can make an educated decision about how many return drivers to include in the asset mix.

You will recall that the main constraint in the PCA process is that each principal component must be *orthogonal*, or completely independent, of all of the others. When applied to investments, PCA finds the underlying factors that drive returns, and those factors are by definition completely uncorrelated to each other. Therefore, we can look at a few portfolios and measure their relative levels of diversification rather easily. Let's define relative diversification:

> **Relative Diversification**: The number of principal components required to explain roughly 75% of the variation in the portfolio.

This is a key concept and can be a very helpful heuristic for analyzing and building portfolios. I hope you retain this concept if nothing else after reading this book.

For the first exercise, we can look at how relative diversification changes as we add assets to the mix. We will start with five assets (Table 5) and work up to the 13 we previously outlined.

Table 5
Portfolio 1 Consisting of Five Investments

Portfolio 1	Five Investments	
US Equity	S&P 500	**SPY**
Non-US Equity	MSCI EAFE	**EFA**
Credit	Barclays US Aggregate Bond Index	**AGG**
Real Estate	DJ US Real Estate Index	**IYR**
Commodity	Bloomberg Commodity Index	**PCRIX**

This is a simple portfolio inspired by Mebane Faber's work in tactical asset allocation. It covers Foreign and Domestic Equities, Bonds, Real Estate, and Commodities with five investments and can serve as a benchmark for a base level of diversification.

The output from a principal component analysis on this portfolio follows. Table 6 shows each of the principal components, which are labeled PC1 to PC5, and the amount of variance explained by each. As mentioned before, the eigenvalue shows the amount of variance explained by a particular eigenvector or principal component.

Wonk Note: The total amount of variation in a sample set is always equal to the number of variables, which, for this example, equals 5. You will note that if you divide the eigenvalue by 5, you will get the Variability (%) you see in the second row of Table 6. PC1 is the first principal component and has an eigenvalue of 3.084. 3.084/5 = 0.61683, or 61.683%.

The cumulative % in Table 6 shows the cumulative amount of variation explained as you add each principal component, and that is where we can find the relative diversification number. In this sample two principal components explain just over 80% of the variation, so we can say that this five asset portfolio has a relative diversification score of 2. (You will see the term *unrotated* in the tables that follow,; this means that the results have not been rotated, which we will do a little later.)

Table 6
PCA Output for Five Investments

Unrotated	PC1	PC2	PC3	PC4	PC5
Eigenvalue	3.084	0.983	0.612	0.237	0.084
Variability (%)	61.683	19.652	12.245	4.746	1.674
Cumulative %	61.683	81.335	93.580	98.326	100.000

Unrotated	PC1	PC2	PC3	PC4	PC5
SPY	0.921	-0.250	-0.149	-0.150	0.211
EFA	0.941	-0.119	0.002	-0.257	-0.188
AGG	0.291	0.950	-0.058	-0.093	0.033
IYR	0.855	0.036	-0.387	0.340	-0.050
PCRIX	0.732	0.048	0.661	0.158	0.022

The bottom part of Table 6 is a loading, or correlation, matrix that shows how each investment loads on each principal component. This is useful because it shows which assets are loading up on the same risk factor and are therefore duplicative from a diversification standpoint. We see that four of the five assets have a very high loading on the first component. Only bonds (AGG) have a low loading on the first component. Typically, a high loading is anything over .500 or .600, depending on the sample. From this analysis, it would appear that real estate (IYR) and commodities (PCRIX) may not add much in terms of diversification because they both have high loadings on the first component. PCRIX is a bit confusing as it has a heavy loading (>0.500) on two components. This happens from time to time, and in a later section, we will see how rotation can often help with situations like this. Now that we have a baseline, we can add assets and see what improvements are possible in terms of relative diversification.

For this example, we are adding five more investments to see how that improves the relative diversification score. In Table 7, you can see that we added US Small Cap and Emerging Market equities, a foreign bond fund, an international real estate fund, and gold. With twice the assets and more international exposure, we should expect some improvement in diversification.

Table 7
10-asset Portfolio

Portfolio 2	10 Investments	
US Equity	S&P 500	**SPY**
Non-US Equity	MSCI EAFE	**EFA**
Credit	Barclays US Aggregate Bond Index	**AGG**
Real Estate	DJ US Real Estate Index	**IYR**
Commodity	Bloomberg Commodity Index	**PCRIX**
US Equity	Russell 2000 Small Cap	**IWM**
Non-US Equity	MSCI Emerging Markets	**EEM**
Credit	Pimco Foreign Bond Fund	**PFORX**
Real Estate	Fidelity International Real Estate Fund	**FIREX**
Commodity	Gold	**GLD**

In the new 10-asset portfolio in Table 8, we get almost to 75% with two components (74.687%). But to be fair, we can go to three principal components, which explains 85% of the variation. Because we were just shy of 75% with two components, we will give this portfolio a relative diversification score of 3. You should also pay attention to the amount of variability explained by each component: in this analysis the first component alone explains 57% of the variability!

Table 8

PCA output for 10 investments

	PC1	PC2	PC3	PC4
Eigenvalue	5.712	1.757	1.051	0.439
Variability (%)	57.118	17.570	10.512	4.393
Cumulative %	57.118	74.687	85.199	89.592
	PC1	PC2	PC3	PC4
SPY	0.916	-0.280	-0.102	-0.005
EFA	0.946	-0.140	0.016	-0.068
AGG	0.272	0.799	-0.345	0.178
IYR	0.830	-0.047	-0.293	0.305
PCRIX	0.718	0.258	0.457	-0.316
IWM	0.870	-0.324	-0.096	0.149
EEM	0.916	-0.094	0.160	-0.070
PFORX	0.372	0.725	-0.378	-0.274
FIREX	0.928	-0.062	-0.058	-0.079
GLD	0.327	0.556	0.668	0.319

By now you may be noticing a pattern: most of the assets tend to load heavily on the first component. I mentioned earlier that the first component explains the largest proportion of the variation possible; so, the first component will tend to identify the biggest risk driver in your collection of investments. You may have also noticed that assets sometimes load on multiple components, and the loadings do not always make intuitive sense. We will discuss later on how to use rotation to clarify the loadings, which can help understand the output a little bit better.

Many investors turn to alternative investments to add diversification to their portfolios. While there are many different kinds of alternatives, for Portfolio 3 in Table 9, we will use three hedge fund indices that track the performance of Long/Short Equity, Event Driven Equity and Managed Futures or CTAs.

Table 9
13 Assets

Portfolio 3	13 Assets	
US Equity	S&P 500	**SPY**
US Equity	Russell 2000 Small Cap	**IWM**
Real Estate	DJ US Real Estate Index	**IYR**
Real Estate	Fidelity International Real Estate Fund	**FIREX**
Non-US Equity	MSCI EAFE	**EFA**
Non-US Equity	MSCI Emerging Markets	**EEM**
Credit	Barclays US Aggregate Bond Index	**AGG**
Credit	Pimco Foreign Bond Fund	**PFORX**
Commodity	Bloomberg Commodity Index	**PCRIX**
Commodity	Gold	**GLD**
Alternative	EurekaHedge Long/Short Equity	**Equity L/S**
Alternative	EurekaHedge Event Driven	**Event Driven**
Alternative	EurekaHedge CTA	**CTA**

Here in Table 10 is the output of the PCA on the 13-asset universe:

Table 10
PCA Output for 13 Assets

	PC1	PC2	PC3	PC4
Eigenvalue	7.312	1.887	1.361	0.641
Variability (%)	56.244	14.514	10.471	4.931
Cumulative %	56.244	70.757	**81.229**	86.160
	PC1	PC2	PC3	PC4
SPY	0.915	-0.254	-0.096	0.069
EFA	0.946	-0.103	-0.029	-0.015
AGG	0.199	0.738	-0.518	0.018
IYR	0.783	-0.056	-0.361	0.026
PCRIX	0.729	0.332	0.278	-0.236
IWM	0.872	-0.301	-0.088	0.042
EEM	0.930	-0.046	0.091	-0.087
PFORX	0.349	0.649	-0.454	0.227
FIREX	0.916	-0.051	-0.137	-0.040
GLD	0.325	0.648	0.404	-0.445
Equity L/S	0.916	-0.104	0.224	0.086
Event Driven	0.910	-0.098	0.128	0.070
CTA	0.190	0.445	0.635	0.553

The results are a bit disappointing: as the relative diversification score did not increase, we can still explain >75% of the variation with three principal components. Nonetheless, two components explain 70%, rather than 75%, and three components now explain 81%, so we can assume diversification was improved a little bit. We found something else of value, as well. Notice that the CTA/Managed Futures Index has effectively no loading on the first principal component and is even lower than bonds, gold, and commodities. We did not increase the relative diversification beyond a score of 3, but we have identified another investment that could bring some meaningful diversification to the portfolio in addition to reducing the variance explained by PCs 1 & 2.

Wonk Note: While we are only showing four principal components, the analysis will actually calculate a larger number: specifically, the number of assets analyzed. In practice, I usually ignore components with eigenvalues of less than 0.50 or so for relative diversification analysis purposes. However, that does not mean that those components are unhelpful from the perspective of identifying investments that could add diversification.

Weighty Matters

The previous examples assume an equal weight allocation to all of the assets in the portfolio. Because most of the assets load very heavily on the first component, which appears to be a proxy for equity risk, nine of the thirteen investments are basically providing the same risk factor—adding more assets with the same risks does not improve diversification, and this analysis demonstrates that. Let's look at what happens if we build and test some rudimentary portfolios.

Portfolio Simulations

We can begin by looking at the base-case portfolio of five different assets. In all portfolio simulations, we will assume an equal weight allocation that is rebalanced monthly unless otherwise specified. Here we can see the performance of the five-asset portfolio over roughly 10 years.

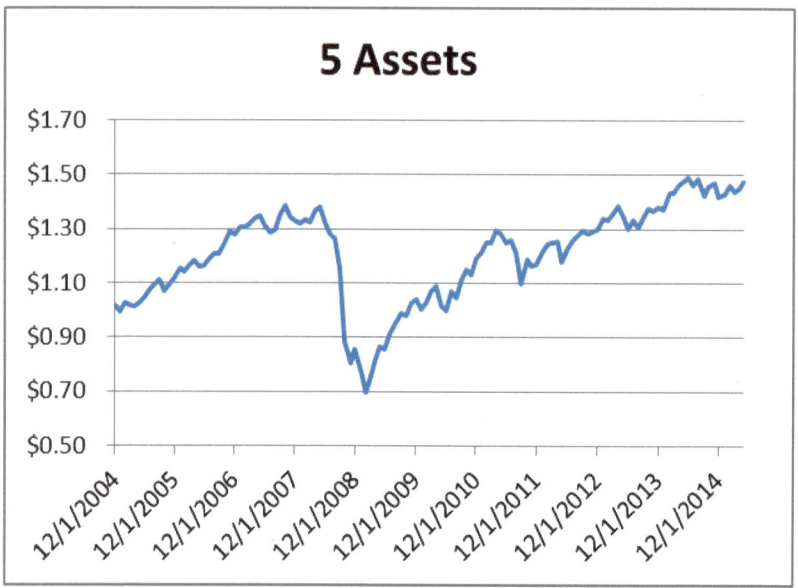

Figure 4. 5-Asset Portfolio Performance

Here in Table 11, we have descriptive statistics for the risk and return of the five-asset portfolio.

Table 11

5-Assets Portfolio Statistics

5-Assets Portfolio Statistics

Cumulative Return	49.78%
AROR	3.77%
Standard Dev.	14.06%
Sharpe Ratio	0.268
CDAR	-12.57%
MAX DD	-49.64%
AROR/CDAR	0.300
AROR/MAXDD	0.076
$1 Becomes	$1.47

While most of the statistics are pretty well known, I should define a few of the less popular ones. CDAR stands for Conditional Drawdown at Risk and is basically the average of the worst n% historical drawdowns. I usually use the worst 5% of drawdowns, and I like to use CDAR in addition to the maximum drawdown to get an idea for how bad drawdowns tend to be. AROR/CDAR and AROR/MAXDD are simply the MAR (AROR/Maximum Drawdown) ratios using annualized rate of return for the entire period and the CDAR or maximum drawdown for the entire period.

We will use this portfolio as our baseline to see how much improvement we get from adding assets and then see whether we can do better by using PCA. Now let's look at the ten asset portfolio. Figure 5 and Table 12 graphically depict the comparison between the two portfolios.

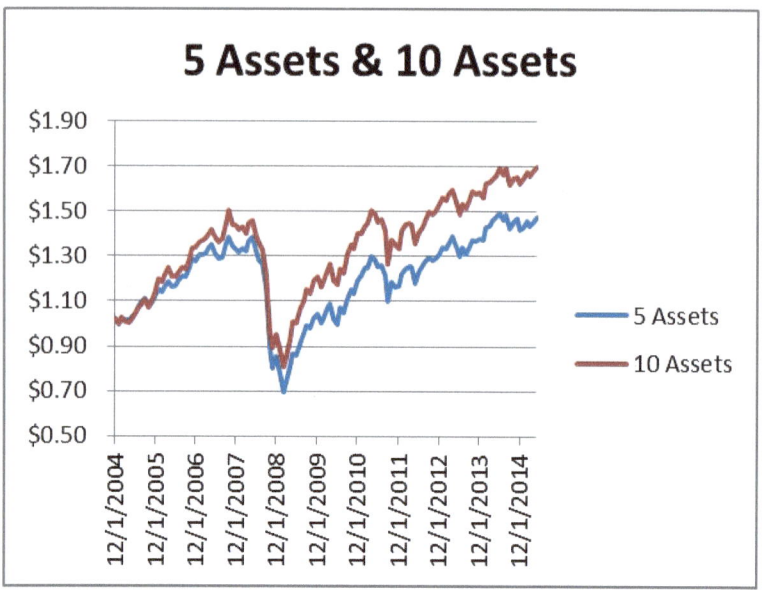

Figure 5. 5- and 10-Asset Portfolios

Table 12
Performance Statistics for 5- & 10-Asset Portfolios

Portfolio Statistics	5 Assets	10 Assets
Cumulative Return	49.78%	63.25%
AROR	3.77%	5.18%
Standard Deviation	14.06%	13.63%
Sharpe Ratio	0.268	0.380
CDAR	-12.57%	-10.27%
MAX DD	-49.64%	-46.25%
AROR/CDAR	0.300	0.504
AROR/MAXDD	0.076	0.112
$1 Becomes	$ 1.47	$ 1.70

There does appear to be some improvement from adding more assets, as the main drawdown in 2008 was smaller, and the 10-assets portfolio generated greater returns. Next, we can look at how the addition of some alternative investments changes things. We look at the performance of three portfolios in Figure 6 and Table 13.

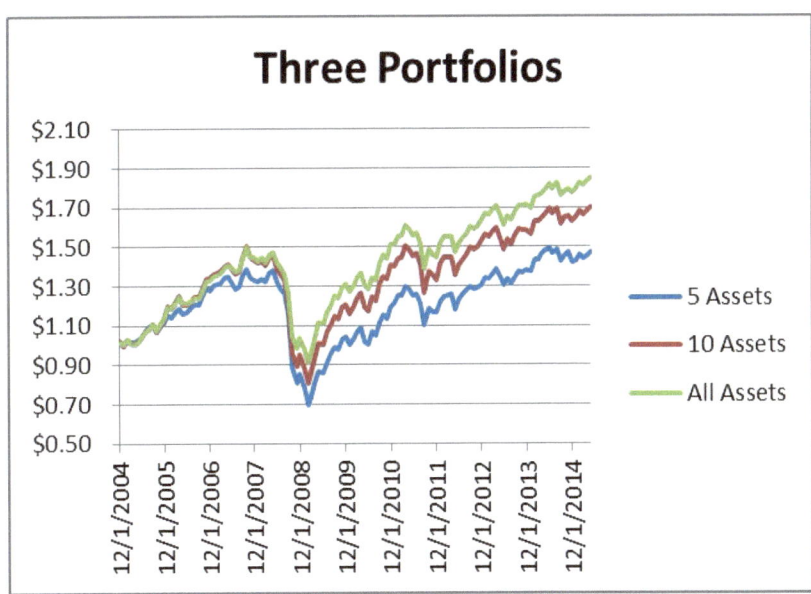

Figure 6: Performance of Three Portfolios

Table 13

Performance Statistics for Three Portfolios

Portfolio Statistics	5 Assets	10 Assets	All
Cumulative Return	49.78%	63.25%	68.86%
AROR	3.77%	5.18%	6.04%
Standard Deviation	14.06%	13.63%	11.56%
Sharpe Ratio	0.268	0.380	0.522
CDAR	-12.57%	-10.27%	-8.21%
MAX DD	-49.64%	-46.25%	-38.92%
AROR/CDAR	0.300	0.504	0.735
AROR/MAXDD	0.076	0.112	0.155
$1 Becomes	$ 1.47	$ 1.70	$ 1.85

Good news! Despite the continued heavy concentration on the first principal component, the 13-assets portfolio turns in better results than the 5- and 10-assets portfolios. Returns increased and all of the risk measures improved. This shows that even modestly uncorrelated assets can add some diversification benefits. Now, let's see if we can use PCA to improve on the 13-assets portfolio.

PCA Portfolio

How can we use PCA to select a portfolio? A simple approach would be to pick one asset that loads heavily on the first component and then consider adding any other assets that do not load heavily on the first component. Let's again examine the PCA output for the 13 asset classes in Table 14.

Table 14
PCA output for 13 assets

	PC1	PC2	PC3	PC4
Eigenvalue	7.312	1.887	1.361	0.641
Variability (%)	56.244	14.514	10.471	4.931
Cumulative %	56.244	70.757	**81.229**	86.160

	PC1	PC2	PC3	PC4
SPY	0.915	-0.254	-0.096	0.069
EFA	0.946	-0.103	-0.029	-0.015
AGG	0.199	0.738	-0.518	0.018
IYR	0.783	-0.056	-0.361	0.026
PCRIX	0.729	0.332	0.278	-0.236
IWM	0.872	-0.301	-0.088	0.042
EEM	0.930	-0.046	0.091	-0.087
PFORX	0.349	0.649	-0.454	0.227
FIREX	0.916	-0.051	-0.137	-0.040
GLD	0.325	0.648	0.404	-0.445
Equity L/S	0.916	-0.104	0.224	0.086
Event Driven	0.910	-0.098	0.128	0.070
CTA	0.190	0.445	0.635	0.553

Nine of the assets in our 13-assets portfolio have high loadings on the first component. One of the highest loadings is for the S&P 500, and since that is a ubiquitous benchmark, we can use that for the representative of the first principal component. Bonds (AGG), Commodities (PFORX), Gold (GLD), and Managed Futures (CTA) have low to very low loadings on the first component.

If we take those five assets, weight them equally, and rebalance monthly (just like we did with the other portfolios), we have the following result shown in Figure 7 and Table 15.

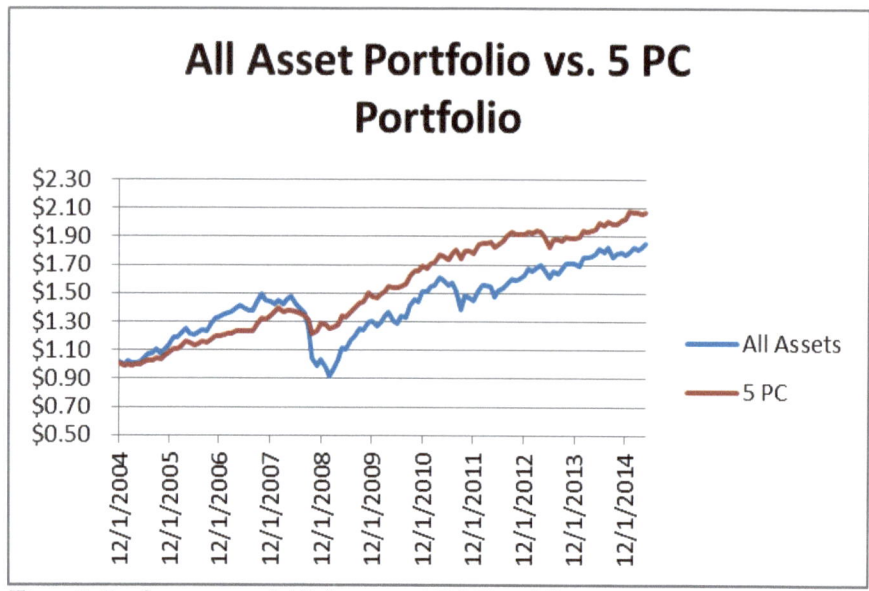

Figure 7. Performance of All Asset and PC Portfolios

Table 15
Portfolio Statistics for All Assets and 5 PCA Assets

Portfolio Statistics	**All Assets**	**5 PCA Assets**
Cumulative Return	68.86%	75.02%
AROR	6.04%	7.19%
Standard Deviation	11.56%	6.02%
Sharpe Ratio	0.522	1.19
CDAR	-8.21%	-0.023
MAX DD	-38.92%	-12.93%
AROR/CDAR	0.735	3.142
AROR/MAXDD	0.155	0.556
$1 Becomes	$ 1.85	$ 2.07

The PCA portfolio handily outstrips the all-asset portfolio in terms of volatility, maximum drawdown, and return, suggesting that we have a much more diversified portfolio despite having fewer investments. We have cut volatility in half and reduced the maximum drawdown by two-thirds and boosted annual return by over 1%. Not bad for running a quick analysis!

In this chapter, we have introduced the concept of relative diversification, shown how to measure relative diversification using PCA, and also demonstrated that by allocating to assets that have loadings on different principal components, we can dramatically increase the diversification and thereby reduce the risk of a multiasset portfolio. In the next chapter, we will look at how rotation can clarify the results of principal component analysis.

4 ROTATION AND STABILITY

In this chapter, we will see how rotating PCA results can make the components clearer and easier to interpret. Then we will apply the analysis to multiple time periods to ensure that PCA is identifying stable relationships.

Rotation

In the previous chapter, we noted that the results of the PCA were unrotated. In simple terms, rotation can be used to wiggle the principal components around in order to maximize each variable's loading on a single component and minimize its loadings on the other components. This can help make the relationships between the assets and the "meanings" of the principal components more clear.

There are different types of rotation, but for our purposes, we want to find independent sources of return, so we will use orthogonal rotation. This will facilitate finding uncorrelated components or factors that will better identify the key return patterns in the data set, which will enhance our ability to identify investments that provide maximum diversification benefits. Varimax rotation is the most popular form of orthogonal rotation, and it rotates the components so that each variable's loadings are maximized on one component and minimized on all of the others. This is ideal for what we want to accomplish, and most PCA packages include Varimax rotation as an option.

Recall the output from the PCA on the 13-asset universe (Table 10) that we used previously. I have presented the original results in Table 16 along with the "rotated" results in Table 17, and I have shown seven components instead of four to give a more complete picture.

Table 16
Factor Loadings for 13 Assets, Un-rotated

	PC1	PC2	PC3	PC4	PC5	PC6	PC7
SPY	0.915	-0.254	-0.096	0.069	-0.090	0.047	0.048
EFA	0.946	-0.103	-0.029	-0.015	-0.065	-0.214	0.013
AGG	0.199	0.738	-0.518	0.018	-0.188	-0.256	-0.031
IYR	0.783	-0.056	-0.361	0.026	-0.337	0.275	0.119
PCRIX	0.729	0.332	0.278	-0.236	0.188	-0.010	0.430
IWM	0.872	-0.301	-0.088	0.042	-0.154	0.219	-0.042
EEM	0.930	-0.046	0.091	-0.087	-0.001	-0.179	-0.097
PFORX	0.349	0.649	-0.454	0.227	0.367	0.204	-0.041
FIREX	0.916	-0.051	-0.137	-0.040	-0.032	-0.207	-0.027
GLD	0.325	0.648	0.404	-0.445	-0.166	0.189	-0.211
Equity L/S	0.916	-0.104	0.224	0.086	0.199	-0.050	-0.158
Event Driven	0.910	-0.098	0.128	0.070	0.285	0.092	-0.095
CTA	0.190	0.445	0.635	0.553	-0.230	-0.016	0.043

Table 17
Factor Loadings for 13 Assets, After Rotation

	PC1	PC2	PC3	PC4	PC5	PC6	PC7
SPY	0.894	0.017	-0.002	-0.042	0.042	0.296	0.113
EFA	0.919	0.154	0.040	0.054	-0.003	0.168	0.172
AGG	0.008	0.929	0.026	0.145	0.323	0.086	0.041
IYR	0.597	0.163	-0.052	0.029	0.140	0.765	0.057
PCRIX	0.505	0.072	0.150	0.329	0.146	0.059	0.764
IWM	0.848	-0.043	-0.031	0.018	0.009	0.403	0.020
EEM	0.905	0.089	0.056	0.175	0.020	0.103	0.175
PFORX	0.134	0.346	0.039	0.086	0.915	0.081	0.090
FIREX	0.870	0.149	-0.028	0.073	0.120	0.206	0.114
GLD	0.110	0.138	0.196	0.947	0.080	0.016	0.163
Equity L/S	0.937	-0.082	0.163	0.120	0.109	-0.021	0.138
Event Driven	0.891	-0.122	0.076	0.097	0.223	0.072	0.190
CTA	0.073	0.023	0.977	0.179	0.033	-0.027	0.077

When you examine the two tables, you see that the loadings have been "focused" to a great extent for each asset, and most assets load heavily on only one component. Our five assets that had low loadings on the first principal component (<0.500) have lower loadings on the first component and tend to load heavily on one single component. US bonds (AGG) is on PC2, International bonds (PFORX) is on PC5, gold (GLD) is on PC4, and managed futures (CTA) is on PC3. In each of these cases, the loadings on other components have been reduced to effectively zero.

There is more we can discover here: as you can see, commodities (PCRIX) and real estate (IYR) had somewhat reduced loadings on the first component and now have their highest loadings on other components. PCRIX has the highest loading on PC7, and IYR has the highest loading on PC6. While they still have relatively high loadings on the first component (> 0.500), the rotation shows that they do have somewhat differentiated return drivers. In the unrotated version, we can see that both US real estate and US small cap equities (IWM) have low yet positive loadings on PC6. In the rotated version, PC6 is the highest loading for IYR, and IWM has a higher loading there, suggesting that there is some commonality between US real estate and US small caps. This is perhaps a non-intuitive result and may be of interest. Commodities (PCRIX) also have a moderate loading on PC4, which has become a proxy for gold.

These nuances in loading patterns can be helpful in a couple of ways. First, they show where the commonalities in returns may be coming from, which is helpful when making allocation decisions. It is also helpful in the case of a portfolio manager managing a single-asset or specialist portfolio.

Multiple Sample Periods

I'll wager that the more experienced quants reading this have been protesting that I broke a pretty major rule in my backtest of the PCA portfolio in the last chapter. The rule I broke was that I used the full data set to perform the analysis and then back tested the portfolios on the same data set. Guilty as charged! The backtest was a simple proof of concept that PCA can identify truly independent sources of returns. The results of PCA tend to be rather stable and do not change a great deal with small changes in inputs. This is good in that it tends to capture long-run, stable relationships between investments. The downside is that PCA is not a good tool for catching changes in these relationships as they are happening. If you are applying PCA to active managers as in allocating to a portfolio of hedge funds, PCA is not necessarily a good tool for identifying "style drift."

In practice, it is a good idea to use as much data as practical for a principal component analysis. But, as I will show in this section, the results are pretty stable and robust to breaking the data into multiple time periods. To do this, I simply split the data into two halves, a little over five years each, and ran a new PCA on each data set, as seen in Tables 18 and 19.

Table 18

PCA Output, First Half of Data, Rotated

First Half	PC1	PC2	PC3	PC4	PC5	PC6
Equity L/S	0.933	0.133	-0.057	0.187	0.184	-0.012
EEM	0.92	0.185	0.137	0.001	0.08	0.133
EFA	0.889	0.092	0.231	0.066	0.028	0.251
Event Driven	0.873	0.097	-0.113	0.363	0.063	0.111
FIREX	0.853	0.073	0.189	0.151	-0.065	0.238
SPY	0.851	-0.038	0.121	0.088	-0.015	0.427
IWM	0.801	-0.049	0.046	0.056	-0.01	0.547
IYR	0.589	0.042	0.129	0.111	-0.1	0.762
PCRIX	0.454	0.318	0.081	0.244	0.163	0.079
PFORX	0.236	0.088	0.363	0.872	-0.024	0.084
GLD	0.123	0.928	0.16	0.078	0.246	0.008
AGG	0.096	0.152	0.941	0.257	-0.028	0.083
CTA	0.076	0.214	-0.028	-0.015	0.968	-0.05

Table 19
PCA Output, Second Half of Data, Rotated

Second Half	PC1	PC2	PC3	PC4	PC5	PC6	PC7	PC8
Equity L/S	0.966	-0.025	0.097	0.101	-0.095	0.008	0.057	-0.092
Event Driven	0.944	-0.025	0.104	0.096	-0.132	-0.013	0.088	-0.136
EFA	0.908	-0.102	0.002	0.082	0.209	0.149	0.186	0.046
EEM	0.883	0.007	0.174	-0.048	0.288	0.105	0.155	0.007
SPY	0.882	-0.100	-0.046	0.081	-0.127	0.301	0.155	-0.151
FIREX	0.871	0.060	0.081	0.056	0.354	0.176	0.154	0.117
IWM	0.845	-0.102	0.102	-0.020	-0.244	0.361	-0.023	-0.167
IYR	0.601	0.232	0.080	0.086	0.055	0.704	0.059	0.181
PCRIX	0.589	-0.017	0.389	0.132	0.036	0.060	0.684	0.083
GLD	0.112	0.121	0.965	0.121	0.008	0.037	0.118	0.075
CTA	0.110	0.159	0.123	0.967	0.003	0.037	0.053	0.071
PFORX	-0.035	0.972	0.090	0.137	0.004	0.058	-0.020	0.145
AGG	-0.208	0.576	0.159	0.147	0.027	0.122	0.067	0.744

The main relationships do not appear to change in the analysis from one period to the next. The four assets with low loadings on the first component remained the same in both samples, and they retained heavy loadings on their own independent components. Real estate and commodities have slightly higher loadings on the first component in the second sample, and US bonds have a somewhat higher loading on the international bonds component (PC2), but they maintain the highest loading on their own component (PC8, which is not shown due to space constraints).

I could have done the analysis on the first half of the data and just run the backtest on the second half of the data, but I really wanted to show at least a ten-year backtest, and there are challenges with getting data for enough assets, especially if you include "alternative" asset classes like hedge funds and managed futures. The data set I selected is easily obtainable from Yahoo for the ETF and mutual fund data and the EurekaHedge website for the alternative investment index data, and that's important. I did not want readers to have to subscribe to an expensive data service in order to replicate these results.

In this chapter, we looked into improving the robustness and depth of our analysis. We saw that rotation—specifically, Varimax rotation—can help to clarify the results of PCA by maximizing the loading of a variable on a single component and minimizing loadings on the other components. Also, I attempted to atone for my sin of using the same data set for the analysis and the backtest in chapter 3 by showing what happens when the data is split. The results showed that PCA does indeed usually pick up on stable relationships, especially where the first component is concerned. In the next chapter, we will walk through implementation of PCA.

5 IMPLEMENTATION

In this chapter, we will work through a more complicated portfolio construction exercise using multiple asset classes. There are many ways to build a portfolio, so please view this as one example and not the only way to proceed. "Bucketing" assets based on their principal component loadings can be helpful in picking assets for a portfolio. In practice, most assets will load on a given component, and you will find that they tend to cluster; however, there will often be a small number of oddballs that do not load heavily on any of the components. For these, I usually create an extra bucket and put all of the oddballs in there.

For this analysis, we are going to use a mostly different set of assets. We are still using 13 (I'm not sure why I keep using that number), but we are using different indices for hedge funds and CTAs, and we are introducing catastrophe bonds into the mix as well. Catastrophe bonds are insurance-linked instruments that resemble high-yield bonds, but they have special provisions for stopping payment or forfeiting the purchase price if a certain type of event happens, such as a hurricane. Because the risks of these instruments are linked to weather or geological events such as earthquakes, they are often considered to be uncorrelated to traditional sources of equity and bond risks.

Using monthly data on stock, bond, equity hedge fund, CTA, and cat bond indices (listed in Table 20) from February 2002 (starting date for the Swiss Re cat bond indices) through October 2012, a PCA was performed and four components were extracted.

Table 20
List of Indices Used for Analysis

SPX	S&P500
MXWO	MSCI World Index
MXEA	MSCI EAFE Index
AGG BOND	Barclays US Aggregate Bond Index
GOV BOND	Barclays US Government Bond Index
BARCSYST Index	Barclay Systematic Trader Index (Trend following)
BARC-CTA	Barclay CTA Index
BTOP50	Barclay BTOP50 Index
HFRIEHI Index	HFRI Equity HF Index
HEDGNAV Index	Dow Jones Credit Suisse Hedge Fund Index
HFN L/S EQUITY	Hedgefund.net Long/short Equity Index
SRCATTRR Index	SwissRe US Cat Bond Total Return Index
SRGLTRR Index	SwissRe Global Cat Bond Total Return Index

Table 21 represents one way to categorize the PCA output for ease of interpretation and as a first step to portfolio construction. First, you review the results and "pick" the component that each asset loads on. You will note that after Varimax rotation, each asset loads on a single component with the mild exception of the Barclays Systematic Trader Index, which is a bit wishy-washy albeit with the heaviest loading on the second component. By regrouping the assets based on their "bucket," which is simply the component number, we can see which assets are similar. One thing that initially jumps out was noted in the previous analysis: stocks and hedge funds are in the same group! If we did a simple equal dollar weight allocation to all 13 assets under consideration, then we would have 6/13 or 46% of our capital allocated to a single risk factor. A table like Table 21 can quickly clarify the risk factors available in portfolio construction while pointing out any risk overlaps.

Table 21
Component Loadings and Buckets, Period of Analysis: 2/2002—10/2012

		Factor loadings after Varimax rotation				
		D1	D2	D3	D4	Bucket
Stocks	SPX	0.909	-0.146	0.097	-0.085	
	MXWO	0.967	-0.082	0.089	-0.044	1
	MXEA	0.963	-0.033	0.075	0.006	
Bonds	AGG BOND	0.024	0.067	0.125	0.977	4
	GOV BOND	-0.281	0.153	0.055	0.933	
CTAs	BARCSYST Index	-0.060	0.547	0.356	-0.061	
	BARC-CTA	0.066	0.948	-0.015	0.137	2
	BTOP50	0.017	0.957	-0.026	0.103	
Equity HFs	HFRIEHI Index	0.963	0.070	0.098	-0.124	
	HEDGNAV Index	0.868	0.258	0.185	-0.045	1
	HFN L/S EQUITY	0.952	0.113	0.093	-0.128	
CAT Bonds	SRCATTRR Index	0.156	0.002	0.972	0.090	3
	SRGLTRR Index	0.161	-0.005	0.970	0.093	

The four components that were extracted represent stocks, bonds, CTAs, and cat bonds. Hedge funds load entirely on the stock component, which is a bit of a surprise because hedge funds are represented by equity long/short indices. The high loadings of the hedge fund indices on the stock component seem to suggest that hedge funds, as measured by the three equity hedge fund indices, would not be a good diversifier for a stock portfolio relative to assets that load on the other components. Aside from the somewhat curious case of equity long/short hedge funds being on the same component as long-only equity indices, the PCA appears to have identified the other distinct asset classes of stocks, bonds, cat bonds, and CTAs.

Because stocks and bonds are usually held in most conventional portfolios, we will look at the effects of adding hedge funds, CTAs, and cat bonds to a base-case stock and bond portfolio of 60% stocks and 40% bonds. Then, we will look at the case of equal-weight portfolios of all asset classes and all asset classes, excluding hedge funds. To test the relative contributions of the various asset classes, we back tested portfolios using various asset mixes. The backtests were performed in the following sequence:

1. An index was created for each asset class by averaging the monthly returns of each index used for that asset (i.e., the three stock index return streams were averaged to create a single stock return stream, and this was done for each of the assets);
2. Portfolio weights were decided on before running the backtest. The base case used 60/40 stocks/bonds and was reduced to 50/30 to allow a 20% allocation to hedge funds, cat bonds, and CTAs in the subsequent backtests. Returns for a given month are computed as follows using equation 4:

   4. $r_m = \sum(r_i * w_i)$

   Where r_m is the monthly return, r_i is the monthly return for a given asset, and w_i is the designated portfolio weight of the asset.

   Finally, equal-weight and equal-weight-excluding hedge fund portfolios were created using an average of the monthly returns for each of the included assets. Return streams were computed in this fashion for the entire period of February 2002 through October 2012 (Figure 8) and a shorter period that ends in December 2008 to see the effects of the financial crisis on the portfolios;
3. Each portfolio was started with a value of $1,000, and the value of the portfolio was computed from month to month using equation 5:

   5. $Value_{t+1} = Value_t * (1 + r_{t+1})$
4. Portfolio returns and risk statistics were computed, and a chart showing the growth of the various portfolios over the entire period was generated based on the values for each of the portfolios over both time horizons. Figure 8 and Table 22 display the results of the backtest, and Table 23 describes the various portfolios simulated.

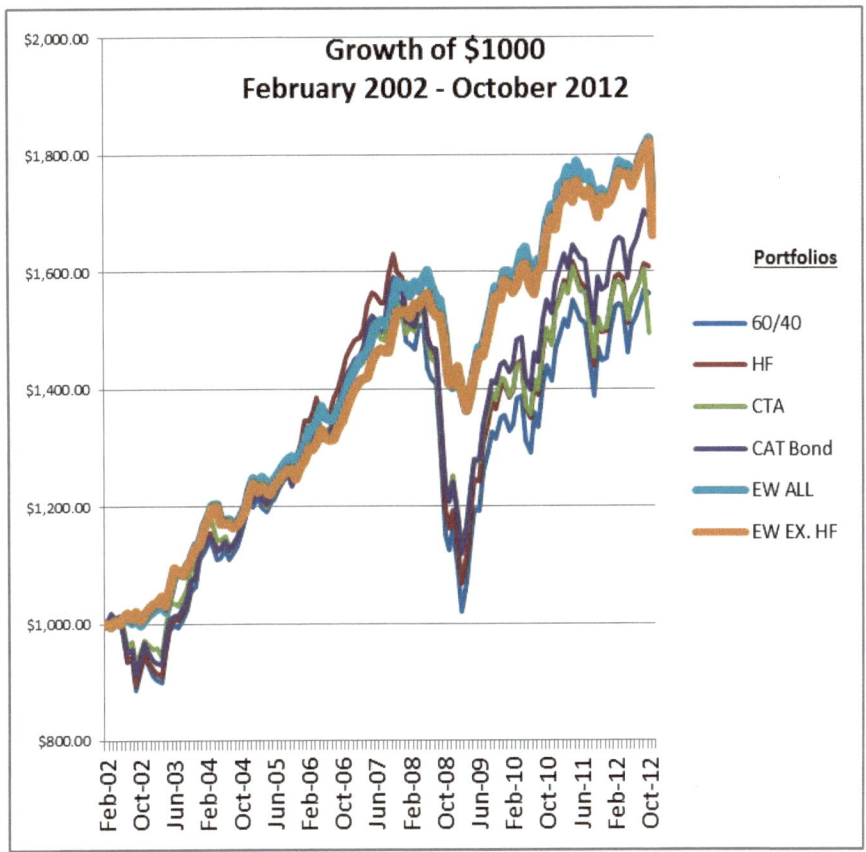

Figure 8. Growth of $1,000 for Each Portfolio

Table 22

Portfolio Statistics for Entire Study Period and Period Ending December 2008

	60/40		HF		CTA		CAT		EW ALL		EW EX. HF	
	All	Dec-08	All	Dec-08	All	Dec-08	All	Dec-08	All	Dec-08	All	Dec-08
AROR	4.24%	2.21%	4.52%	2.60%	3.81%	3.32%	5.03%	3.19%	5.07%	5.29%	4.85%	5.40%
STDEV	9.86%	8.97%	9.48%	8.71%	8.59%	7.50%	8.39%	7.67%	5.50%	4.75%	5.48%	4.41%
CDAR	-8.48%	-5.79%	-8.31%	-5.77%	-6.10%	-3.98%	-6.46%	-4.66%	-2.84%	-2.14%	-2.49%	-1.94%
MAXDD	-35.30%	-28.67%	-34.45%	-28.70%	-28.13%	-22.24%	-29.75%	-24.04%	-14.83%	-12.40%	-12.72%	-9.89%

Table 23
Descriptions of Portfolios

Portfolio Descriptions	
60/40	60/40 STOCKS AND BONDS
HF	50/30/20 STOCKS, BONDS, AND HEDGE FUNDS
CTA	50/30/20 STOCKS, BONDS, AND CTAs
CAT	50/30/20 STOCKS, BONDS, AND CAT BONDs
EW ALL	EQUAL-WEIGHT OF ALL ASSETS
EW EX. HF	EQUAL WEIGHT OF ALL ASSETS, EXCLUDING HEDGE FUNDS

The results demonstrate that during the period studied, hedge funds did not provide meaningful diversification to the stock and bond portfolio, but CTAs and cat bonds did provide meaningful diversification. This is in agreement with what the PCA suggested because hedge funds were on the same component as stocks, suggesting very similar return streams and drivers. CTAs and cat bonds decreased the risk of the stock and bond portfolio by meaningful amounts. The portfolio using CTAs had less risk during both periods, but it had lower returns than stocks and bonds alone during the full-time period and higher returns through the crisis period (ending December 2008). The cat bond portfolio had higher returns and lower risk in both periods. The stock/bond/hedge fund portfolio had slightly higher returns and slightly lower risk for both periods than the stock/bond portfolio alone, but these differences were not meaningful as they were far less than 1%.

A 20% allocation to CTAs and cat bonds had good results for the stock and bond portfolio, but the clear winner for the entire period in this backtest was a simple equal-weight portfolio of all of the assets studied: stocks, bonds, hedge funds, CTAs, and cat bonds. If hedge funds were excluded from the backtest and there was simply an investment in an equal-weight portfolio of stocks, bonds, CTAs, and cat bonds, the portfolio would have outperformed through December 2008 and lagged somewhat over the entire period.

PCA has once again identified distinct return streams and showed that equity long/short hedge funds would not provide meaningful diversification benefits to a portfolio that already included stocks. Adding CTAs and cat bonds decreased the risk of the portfolios without detriment to the returns, and an equal-weight allocation across all of the asset classes had the best return and the lowest risks. The equal-weight portfolio, at least during the period of this study, did the best job of maintaining wealth for the investor, which is easily seen in Figure 8.

In this chapter, we performed several simulations using commodity trading advisors, hedge funds, and fixed-income indices to determine if principal component analysis can identify diversifiable risks in an investment opportunity set or portfolio by assisting an investor in identifying investments with the ability to enhance portfolio diversity. In each simulation, statistically and economically significant improvements were generated by using PCA factors for diversification purposes. These results present strong evidence that PCA can be used to create better diversified portfolios, to provide better understanding of the risks in a portfolio or investment universe, and to identify investments that load on factors that are orthogonal to the majority of the portfolio allocations. Fund managers seeking better risk-adjusted returns for their multiasset portfolios can benefit from this tool, as seen in the multiasset example.

CONCLUSION AND SUMMARY

In this short book, I have attempted to demonstrate that PCA can be used to identify risks in multiple dimensions and that this can be a helpful tool for improving portfolio selection and diversification.

First in Chapter 1, we looked at challenges to using correlations when building portfolios. In Chapter 2, I introduced PCA and walked through how it works. In Chapter 3, I defined the key concept of Relative Diversification as the required number of principal components (which represent orthogonal risk factors) to explain 75% of the variation in a portfolio. We then saw that adding more investments does not necessarily improve diversification and that the 13-asset portfolio could be "beaten" by a 5-asset portfolio selected using insights from our principal component analysis. In Chapter 4, I showed how rotation can clarify the results of PCA and attempted to atone for my backtesting sins by showing that PCA results tend to be robust over multiple time frames. Finally in Chapter 5, we went through a portfolio construction exercise, using PCA to build and test various portfolios from the ground up and show how we could drastically reduce risks while maintaining solid returns.

APPENDIX I: PORTFOLIO UPDATE

2015 was a rocky year—how did our 5-asset portfolio hold up? You will recall that an equal weight portfolio of five assets selected using PCA beat a 13-asset portfolio from 2004 through 2014, especially in terms of greatly reducing volatility and drawdowns. Although one year, or 12 months, is a very small sample, our little model portfolio held up well in 2015. Both portfolios lost money in 2015; however, the 5-PCA asset portfolio lost less money with lower volatility and a smaller drawdown mid-year. This result suggests that the 5-asset portfolio continues to have better diversification than the broader 13-asset portfolio. Due to the short window of time, I did not include Sharpe or other ratios because I don't think they are very meaningful for a 12-month time period.

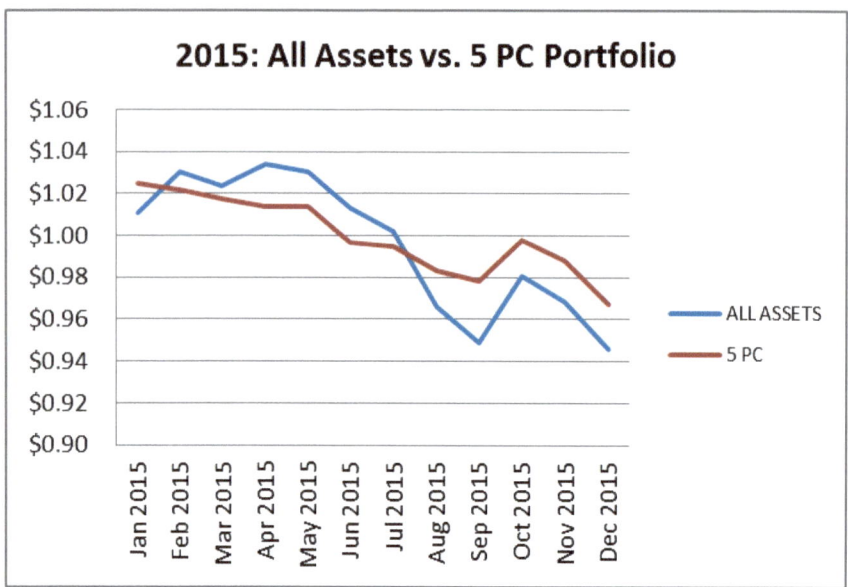

Figure 9. 2015 Performance

Table 23
Portfolio Statistics for 2015

	All Assets	PCA 5
2015 Return	-5.38%	-3.25%
Standard Deviation	6.8%	4.6%
Max Drawdown	-8.52%	-5.61%
$1 Becomes	$ 0.95	$ 0.97

APPENDIX II: PCA PROCESS OUTLINE

The details of how you perform the analysis will vary based on your investment universe and the software you are using, but most of the steps generalize to any universe or software package. The following are the steps in the PCA process:

I. Select universe of investments—be sure to select investments with a sufficient amount of historical returns.
II. Collect data.
III. Clean data:
    a. Make sure all of the returns have the same frequency;
    b. Identify and deal with missing values;
    c. Convert the frequency of data (I typically use weekly data), if necessary.
IV. Save clean data as separate files: I recommend two versions, one as a backup and one to feed into the software.
V. Perform the analysis:
    a. Use the correlation matrix unless you have a good reason not to;
    b. Use varimax rotation;
    c. Let the analysis return a relatively large number of components—don't feel you have to limit the results to a certain number or use a harsh criterion for retaining components.
VI. Review results.

ADDITIONAL RESOURCES

Software

R: R is an open source statistical computing environment. The Psych package can do PCA, and the GPA Rotation package can apply Varimax rotation. www.r-project.org

XLStat: A statistical add-in for MS Excel that has a comprehensive PCA function. Not free. www.xlstat.com

Books

Alexander, C. (2008). *Practical financial econometrics* (Market risk analysis, Volume II). Chichester, UK: Wiley.

Dunteman, G. (1989). *Principal components analysis*. Thousand Oaks, CA: Sage.

ABOUT THE AUTHOR

Dr. Rufus Rankin is a portfolio manager and the Director of Research of Equinox Institutional Asset Management. Dr. Rankin holds a BA in Philosophy and a Masters in International Studies from North Carolina State University, and a Doctorate of Business Administration (Finance) from Grenoble Ecole de Management.

www.ingramcontent.com/pod-product-compliance
Lightning Source LLC
Chambersburg PA
CBHW040852180526
45159CB00001B/403